Tips, Tricks and Cheats
for over 40 Moshi Mini Games

SUNBIRD

Published by Ladybird Books Ltd 2011
A Penguin Company
Penguin Books Ltd, 80 Strand, London, WC2R 0RL, UK
Penguin Books (USA) Inc., 375 Hudson Street, New York 10014, USA
Penguin Books Australia Ltd, Camberwell Road, Camberwell, Victoria 3124,
Australia (A division of Pearson Australia Group Pty Ltd)
Penguin Group (NZ), 67 Apollo Drive, Rosedale, Auckland 0632,
New Zealand (a division of Pearson New Zealand Ltd)
Canada, India, South Africa

Sunbird is a trade mark of Ladybird Books Ltd

Written by Oli Smith

www.ladybird.com

ISBN: 978-1-40939-052-7
001 - 10 9 8 7 6 5 4 3 2 1
Printed in China

Contents

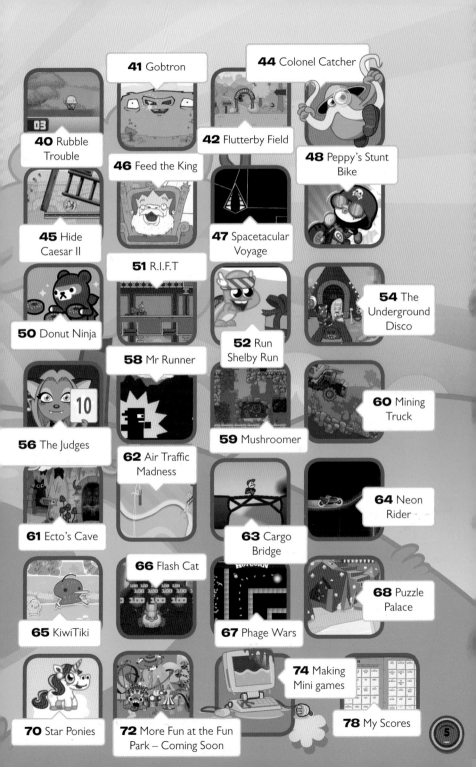

Game On!

Puzzle Palace

Moshi Fun Park

Flutterby Field

MONSTRO City

Moshling Boshling

Hey there Moshi gamers! I'm **Raarghly** - the owner of the **Games Starcade**. I've played every game on Moshi Island and I always like to wander the Fun Park to see what new games the Roarkers have come up with and check if anyone's beaten my high scores!

From the Puzzle Palace's Daily Challenges, to making ice cream with Giuseppe Gelato, I've made it my mission to discover the moves that lead to those **perfect scores** (I've even braved the glare of Simon Growl's hair whilst showing off my "tentacle two-step" in the Underground Disco).

Games Starcade

En-Gen

Inside this book you'll find guides to dozens of my favourite games, complete with tips on where to find them, how to play them and the characters you'll meet along the way. I've even added some **handy hints** on how to boost your score for every game and a section at the back to record your First Scores and High Scores!

You can also check out my guide to making Mini Games at the back of the book. I've spoken to many Roarkers during my trips to the Fun Park, and they've let me in on the secrets to what makes a good game great - you never know, one day I might be writing about one of your games!

Anyway, stop listening to me. Log on to **MoshiMonsters.com**, choose a game and get playing - I could do with the competition!

Game on!

Raarghly

"Look, it's me!"

Raarghly is a monster from another world. Which world? Nobody knows. Flying around Monstro City in his mini flying saucer, Raarghly **loves to help players** settle into their new homes and teach them how to take care of their monsters. But when he's not helping others, he can always be found indulging in his other passion - playing games!

You can find Raarghly in his shop, the **Games Starcade**, where he sells Starcade machines to other monsters to decorate their rooms.

Raarghly's so good at games that he can play six at a time, and he's always looking for **other monsters to compete with** in the hope that one of them can beat him! It's lonely at the top of the high scores - so he's always keen to help others improve their skills, giving them hints and tips on how to get as many points as possible.

Frazzled!

Oh no! A lightning bolt has zapped the Games Starcade, sizzled Raarghly's prices and scrambled all his machines! Can you help him fix the damage by unscrambling the names of each Starcade machine and writing down how much they cost?

"If you don't know the answer, the next few pages should help you to help me!"

___Roxx

coto's

ceo teenurdav

_ _ _ _ ' _   _ _ _   _ _ _ _ _ _ _ _ _

_ _ _ ' _   _ _ _   _ _ _ _ _ _

___Roxx

gub's gib

nocube

leview linekev

___Roxx

wondlilh hads

_ _ _ _ _ _ _   _ _ _ _ _ _ _

_ _ _ _ _ _ _ _   _ _ _ _

___Roxx

ase sotnerm

chumn

_ _ _   _ _ _ _ _ _ _ _   _ _ _ _ _

9

Octo's Eco Adventure

Use the mouse to aim Octo's blowhole and **squirt the trash** falling from the sky before it hits the water. Bin bags, tyres, dustbins and even old boots are falling, all at **different speeds**! If four things hit the water, then you'll get sent back to the start! Things getting hectic? Luckily, there are some helpful stars that will give you a steady **burst of shots** for a limited period of time!

RAARGHLY'S TIPS

"Anticipation is the key here - try to aim the target just below the falling trash so that it falls into the water burst. Different rubbish falls at different speeds so aim it even further below for the faster-moving objects."

"The Star power-up allows Octo to fire a steady stream of water, so when you get it keep the left mouse button held down and go crazy! This is especially helpful when there is lots of falling rubbish as you can create a barrier for it all to fall into."

"Potion Ocean needs protecting, and who better to do it than Octo? Help her on her mission to keep the shores of Monstro City clean for only 700 Rox!"

Octo

Octo is the queen of the water and you can find her living large in the Port! She's the spouter and spritzer of fine, fresh mist and our eco-conscious **water recycler**, clearing the waters around Moshi Island of rubbish so that her fishy friends can swim safely in the beautiful coral reefs. On a nice day, she'll give you a spray that beats even the best bath!

Raining Rubbish

Octo's working overtime to protect Potion Ocean from the falling rubbish, but she's always keen to know how much work she's done. Each piece of rubbish is worth a different number of eco-points. Add them up using the chart below to find out Octo's eco-total!

+ 2

- 3

+ 5

+ 7

- 4

+1

Bug's Big Bounce

This game might look simple, but **careful planning** is required to reach the highest clouds in the sky!

Use the mouse to **guide Bug's jumps** so that he lands on the clouds, using them as a springboard to jump even higher. Keep an eye out for the **extra-bouncy rainbows** that can boost you even further. Be careful of the rainclouds - one jump and they will disappear for good.

RAARGHLY'S TIPS

"Remember that Bug can jump all the way across the screen with a swipe of the mouse. Sometimes a quick jump to the side can open up a whole new route upwards."

"Use the rain clouds wisely. Sometimes they'll be the only way to progress and a mistimed jump can send you plummeting back towards the ground. Try not to use them if you don't have to. Leaving the rainclouds where they are can provide a handy safety bounce if you miss a jump further up."

"The rainbows can help you cover huge distances, so don't be afraid to drop down a little way to use one. Their boost will more than make up for it!"

"Is it a bird? Is it a plane? No, it's Bug! For only 500 Rox you and your friends can help Bug in his quest to find the top of the sky!"

Bug

It is said that if monsters were supposed to fly, then they would have been given wings. But Bug doesn't listen to that. In fact, he doesn't listen much at all! Together with his best friend Ratty, Bug is always getting himself in trouble. Whether it's rearranging dino bones over at the Unnatural History Museum or stealing Pepperbombs from The Pepperbomb Geyser . . . You'll always find him up to no good.

Reach for the Sky

Help Bug reach the rainbow by drawing him a path through the clouds.

Bug can only travel three dots in any direction with each jump, and each jump must end on a cloud! There is only one safe route to the rainbow - can you find it?

Sea Monster Munch

Sea Monster Munch is easy to learn, but to get those really high scores you need to be very careful indeed.

Use the arrow keys to **guide the Sea Monster** to its next meal, whilst being careful not to collide with the rocky sides or the ocean floor. As it eats, the Monster will get longer. **Be careful** that it doesn't begin to eat its own tail!

On the medium and harder difficulties, your reflexes will need to be lightning-quick, as the Sea Monster **moves much faster** - but each meal is also worth more points.

RAARGHLY'S TIPS

"Don't be afraid to take the long way around. As the Monster's tail grows, it's important to keep it out of the way so that an accidental change of direction doesn't spell game over. Moving in the opposite direction of your next meal before turning around to snap it up makes sure your tail is out of the way."

"Help the Sea Monster find its food - but watch out for its tail as it grows! For only 850 Rox you can challenge your friends to see who can make it eat the most."

Sea Monster

Lurking in the shadows beneath the waves, the deadly Sea Monster coils itself, **ready to spring** upon its next unfortunate victim . . . well, not really. Sea Monster is actually quite a **friendly creature** - it's not his fault he needs to eat fish! He's also rather clumsy, always tripping over his own tail, and whilst this might overturn the odd fishing boat, he's always careful to put everything back where he found it!

The Terrible Tangle

Sea Monster has gone and got himself tangled up again! But only one of these knots is made up of a single Sea Monster - can you spot which one?

Downhill Dash

Test Weevil Kneevil's **stunt-driving skills** by using the arrow keys to weave a path down the slope.

This game is all about **collecting stars**. You'll need to weave across all three lanes to get the highest score possible. Ramps will catapult you into the air and fallen logs or oil spills will stop you in your tracks. Be careful: it only takes **two crashes** to end the game, so keeping an eye on what's coming up is important!

Red stars give you 10 points, whilst silver stars give you 100 and gold 500. Plan your route carefully to **maximise your score!**

RAARGHLY'S TIPS

"Although there are a lot of stars on the ground, most of the higher scoring ones can only be reached using the ramps. Often it's worth missing a few stars to catch some air and some extra points!"

"If you manage to last long enough without a crash, Kneevil's bike will pick up speed and eventually earn a boost! Whilst this makes your jumps longer, it's also much more difficult to avoid obstacles."

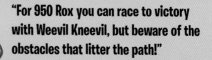

"For 950 Rox you can race to victory with Weevil Kneevil, but beware of the obstacles that litter the path!"

Weevil Kneevil

Weevil Kneevil is **Main Street's only courier**, mostly because he's the only monster who can ride safely through the crowds of shoppers! He delivers parcels between Yukea and Bizarre Bazaar. Some whisper that he's delivering love letters between the shop keepers, but Weevil swears it's only his prize-winning pickled blueberry rings.

A **born daredevil**, Weevil is always on the lookout for places to practise his stunts. He can often be seen hurtling through the air on his bike in search of a safe place to land!

The Rickety Tower

Weevil is preparing for his greatest stunt yet, but he's not sure his tower will hold with all these gaps in it! Help him choose the four objects that will slot into the gaps before the pile comes crashing down to the ground!

1

2

3

4

A B C D E F G H I J K L

17

Raining Cats and Dogs

Use your mouse to **keep the skydiver falling** steadily, with the help of some flying aliens and friendly cats. Look out for the evil spiky purple creatures and the vampire bats, who want to bring you crashing down to Earth with a bump.

Landing on the friendly aliens will not only break your fall but also give you **100 points** each. Create combos by bursting them in quick succession.

To help you even further, landing on a cat will fill the screen with aliens. This makes it easier to fall safely and also helps you rack up even more points!

But there are some less friendly creatures as well. The spiky purple aliens won't help to break your fall, whilst the vampire bats will give you a nasty nip that will send you falling straight to the '**Game Over**' screen.

umutdervis.com ©2016

its raining
Cats & Dogs!

start game
instructions
more games

Presented by...

-- Instructions --

Use your mouse and fall at a constant rate as much as possible. Don't reach the bottom of the screen!

Land on these creatures to cut your speed.

Beware of these creatures!

doesn't slow   It bites you!

cat

21700

"As you progress through the levels, your speed will increase even further. Make sure you grab every cat you can get to keep your diver bouncing!"

Jump'It

As evening falls over an unknown city, a lone man decides to go for a run across the rooftops. Help him **find a safe path** over the skyscrapers and scaffolding, where deadly drops threaten to end his exercise for good!

The runner always runs at the same speed and it's up to you to **time his jumps** so that he lands safely on the next platform. Use the X key or space bar to jump to safety.

"Like the runner's speed, his jumps are always the same distance, so it's important to make sure you time his leaps carefully. Jump too soon and he could miss the drop altogether. With the smaller platforms, a late jump could mean he overshoots completely!"

"Your runner never starts the game in the same place, so get ready for some surprise leaps of faith every time you start!"

"Try not to hold down the jump button. If you do, the runner will keep jumping and often miss his next platform!"

YOUR FINAL SCORE: **6580**

PRESS [SPACE] TO PLAY AGAIN

© Sandeep Saha

Ozee

Help a young explorer navigate the mind-bending puzzles and **treacherous traps** of this woodland world to gain stars!

Using the arrow keys to walk and jump, the A key to run and the S key to pull, push and activate switches, you must **navigate the environmental puzzles** with careful planning and even more careful timing. Rolling balls, tumbling blocks and timed challenges are just some of the obstacles you'll encounter on your journey. Soon you'll be **stringing moves together** to perform astonishing acrobatic feats. Keep an eye out for helpful diagrams to give you hints on how to progress: and remember, what goes up must always come down.

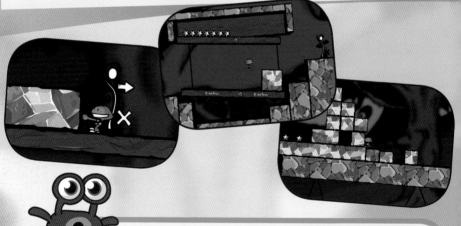

"If you get stuck, don't be afraid to press the R key. This will take you back to the most recent checkpoint and reset the puzzle so you can have another go!"

"Remember to take one last look around before leaving a level. There is often a final puzzle for those who take the time to explore, which will reward you with a shower of stars!"

"If you're heading for a fall, don't forget that you can use the S key to grab onto things and save yourself!"

Solipskier

In a black and white world, your daredevil skier must **race and trick** his way across a landscape drawn by you.

Holding down the mouse button and dragging it across the screen will **create a path** for the skier to travel across. Create hills and valleys to increase his speed. Be sure to guide him through the high-scoring gateways and tunnels he'll encounter along the way.

Bonus point multipliers are awarded for taking risks, and letting go of the mouse button causes the skier to do a variety of airborne tricks. Make sure you give him a safe place to land when he finishes!

"Even more multipliers are awarded if your skier passes through a gate whilst airborne!"

"The faster your skier is going, the further he will travel through the air, giving him more time to trick before he lands."

"The length of the skier's rainbow tail will tell you how long you have left to do another trick before you lose your multiplier."

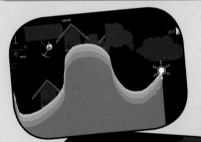

© Mikengreg

Moshling Boshling

"When the picnickers on Main Street have their cakes stolen by **Dr. Strangeglove**'s latest creations, there's only one team you can call - the **Super Moshis!**"

From the meadows outside the Fun Park to Main Street and beyond, those greedy Glumps aren't going to return the Moshlings' cakes without a fight. You'll need to **fire your friends** from a giant catapult to demolish their makeshift fortresses. Hold down the mouse button and drag your Moshlings to prepare the catapult. Let go to send them soaring into the air. Choose your angles carefully to cause the maximum amount of damage and **squash all the Glumps** to complete each level.

If that wasn't challenging enough, there are also three cakes hovering in the air on every map. You'll need your Moshlings to catch them all to get the maximum amount of Rox. Each cake is worth 10 Rox so be sure not to leave any behind!

Super Projectiles:

As your war with the Glumps continues, they'll begin to create even sturdier structures to shelter in. Luckily, you'll gain access to a group of super-powered Moshlings with special abilities to take them down!

Click whilst Tiki and Peppy are in the air to give them an extra burst of speed. Use them to fine-tune your aim, break through barriers or simply travel further across the map.

Clicking Gurgle will cause him to dive-bomb - great for picking off those Glumps hiding behind walls.

Super Furi is incredibly strong. Fire him at stone structures to break through and clear a path for the weaker Moshlings to follow.

Blurp will explode if you click him whilst in the air - but remember, it will take him a few seconds to detonate so time your clicks carefully. If he hits anything the timer will begin automatically.

RAARGHLY'S TIPS

"Follow the cakes! Sending your Moshlings on a course to retrieve those delicious treats will often position them in the perfect place to take down more Glumps!"

"You have to fire your Moshlings in a certain order and there's often only a few ways to take out every Glump. Look at the map carefully to see which Glumps can only be taken out by certain Moshlings. Don't waste a Gurgle on an easy one just because it's up first!"

"Chain reactions are good, and you can often take out all the Glumps using only a few of the Moshlings available. Take out the supports of any larger towers to send them tumbling down in all directions, leaving you to mop up the cakes with the leftover Moshlings!"

Ice Scream!

For your first few days at the parlour, Giuseppe keeps things easy for you, but soon you'll be **juggling more flavours, toppings, sauces and cones** than you can keep track of! As word spreads of your Ice Scream skills, the customers will ask for more and more elaborate combinations. It'll be up to you to keep them happy before time runs out! If you impress Giuseppe enough, he'll ask you to help expand his business, taking his ice cream cart to the beach and even inside a volcano - helping monsters cool down wherever they are.

There are four slots for creating your ice creams in the centre of the screen. You need to drag and drop the toppings and sauces into place according to each customer's order. If you do it quickly enough, they **might give you a tip**, but get it wrong or leave them waiting too long and they'll leave without paying at all!

Giuseppe will give you a **target** to reach each day. If you fail to beat it the first time, don't worry. He'll give you two more chances before asking you to start from the beginning.

"Poor old Giuseppe Gelato, his Ice Scream Parlour is so popular, he's having trouble serving everyone! Help him out by creating spectacular treats for every customer!"

"Don't forget to click the Rox on the counter to collect them. If you don't do it before the time runs out, they won't count towards your final score!"

"It's easy to plan ahead during the first few days. Fill your tray with cones and fill them with a scoop of each colour. After that, all you have to worry about is getting the right toppings to each customer and collecting those tips!"

"Keep an eye on the customers' moods. If you give them their ice scream while their mood is green, they'll tip you. If not, it might be better to serve someone who will first."

"At the higher levels, it's almost impossible to fulfil every order. Try to do the most elaborate recipes first as they pay the most Rox!"

"If you accidentally make the wrong combination, just drag the cone to the trash to clear some space."

CE-SCREAM!

Giuseppe Gelato

Giuseppe Gelato owns the Ice Scream store on Ooh La Lane, but can also be found wheeling his cart around Monstro City, hoping to catch a few sun-kissed monsters in need of some cooling off!

He is so eager to serve the next customer that he often tells others to scram before they get served. But Giuseppe's ice creams are so good that they always come back to see what new toppings he's whipped up in his kitchen.

He's always in need of a helping hand, so drop in to earn a few Rox!

Orders Up!

Giuseppe's got loads of customers, but not enough ice cream to serve them all! Which two customers can he serve with the ingredients he has, to earn the most Rox?

Orders:

A.

15 Rox

B.

5 Rox

C.

10 Rox

D.

8 Rox

E.

13 Rox

F.

7 Rox

Available Ingredients:

Hanna in a Choppa

Hanna's got a new helicopter and needs you to help her put it to good use!

Use the arrow keys to **steer the Choppa** through each level, and the Z and X keys to rotate in mid-air. With these skills and your trusty winch (activated by pressing the space bar), Hanna is more than ready to face the **twenty-one challenges** that confront her, from squashing bees, to herding sheep and saving shipwrecked sailors!

But beware: your Choppa can only take so much of a beating before it crashes. You'll have to be a careful flier to reach the flag that marks the end of every level.

FLY THIS TO THIS
WITH THESE BRING IT ON!
(c'mon, clicky cli...)

DEPOSIT FOUR SHEEP TO UNLOCK EXIT

"Even if you are a whizz at completing your chopper mission, there are loads of other bonus achievements to try and pick up as well! Try completing each level without touching the sides or doing it super-fast! There are also more specific mission achievements. Click on 'Display Achievements' in the mission menu screen to check them out!"

"Be careful with your winch - fly too fast and you could end up being spun around by your cargo!"

© Deeper Beige

Skywire 2

Take your pixel passengers on a ride through a jigsaw world! Use the up and down arrow keys to control the **speed and direction** of your cable car and bring them safely to the end of each course.

Of course, things aren't as simple as they seem. There are various creatures along each route that are **keen to spoil the journey**. Hit one and a passenger will fall out. If you lose all three, you'll need to retry the level. Your time score is multiplied by the number of passengers who reach the end of each level, so try to keep as many as safe as possible to achieve the maximum amount of points!

You can also play Skywire 2 with **two players** on the same keyboard. The second player uses the W and S keys to move. Each half of the screen will show a ghost of your opponent, so you can track their progress.

© Nitrome

"Watch out for momentum! It takes a while to brake the cable car so be careful how you adjust your speed, especially on the loopier sections of track! If you hit a creature, the car will become invincible for a few seconds, so take advantage of that to get as far as possible."

"You'll get higher scores for travelling slower and keeping all your passengers than getting to the end as quickly as possible with just one. Take the time to learn each creature's moves before you try to pass them."

Pumpkins

All the fun of **carving pumpkins** without the mess! Select and drag cut-out shapes from the left-hand menu and filled shapes from the right. Then use the mouse tools to rotate and change their size and position on the pumpkin face. The star symbol on both sides allows you to **create your own shapes** just by clicking an outline onto the pumpkin. Click back to the start to cut it out (or fill it in if you're using the right-hand tool).

Don't worry if you make a mistake. Simply double-click the pumpkin at the bottom of the screen to reset your carving. When you're done, you can click 'view' to admire your handiwork or even **print your design!**

Press the button down there to start carving!

Click and drag to rotate the shape.
Click and drag to resize it.

Click and drag to rotate the shape.
Click and drag to resize it.

"Shapes overlap, so try combining more than one and changing their sizes and angles to create more complex designs."

"Whilst viewing your finished design, move your mouse around the pumpkin to view it from different angles."

© **Reptangle**

Donut Dance

These colourful bears are rather cheeky, and like to pass their leader's **precious donut** between themselves whilst they dance. Follow the donut as the dance progresses and click on the last bear holding the donut to **expose them**! Get it wrong and the correct bear will keep it for itself.

Tappi Bear Series 02

Donut Dance

Start Help App Store

Tap the bear who hold the donut

Remember the last donut location and tap the bear.

Start Help App Store

TOP SCORE 033 SCORE 009

Dance

TOP SCORE 033 SCORE 008

"The more donuts you find, the harder this game gets. You'll need a keen eye to keep track, as the bears pass the donut faster and more often!"

Snowdrift

Help the yeti **navigate the frozen wastes** by using the arrow or W, A, S and D keys to move, jump and slide. Collect penguins to increase your score, but watch out for King Penguins, rocket-firing foxes, grenade-throwing bears and other enemies.

As the game progresses the environment will become **more treacherous**. Spikes, rotating blocks and other hazards will litter your path. The yeti can take three hits before he needs to restart the level and you can **replenish his health** by collecting fish along the way.

"Enemies can only be killed by sliding into them, but taking them out doesn't add to your score. Don't be afraid to simply jump over them to progress."

"If an enemy isn't standing on a patch of ice, you'll be unable to kill them, so keep an eye on the terrain!"

"Tilting platforms pivot in the middle, so try to land there to avoid slipping off!"

"Explore! Bonus penguins can often be found just off the main path."

Thin Ice

Monsters have **invaded** your skater's frozen pond and it's up to you to remove them!

Your skater will always move towards the mouse and leaves behind a crack in the ice as he does so. Use it to **cut holes** in the ice for the monsters to drop through by looping your skater around them before time runs out. Be careful not to fall into the holes yourself. Your skater only has a limited amount of energy and collisions with monsters or drops into the frozen water will gradually wear it down. Collect **special power-ups** and bonus points around the pond to improve your chances against the monsters.

"The crack that trails the skater gradually fades, so you'll need to draw small loops around each monster to create a hole."

"Hitting a monster causes your skater to rebound and will often prevent you from completing a circle - so skate carefully!"

"Remember that once the last monster has fallen through the ice, the level ends. Make sure you pick up every bonus before finishing off that last enemy!"

"Monsters won't walk into holes you've created, but you will! Move between opposite sides of the pond as you take out monsters to avoid the holes you've made until they thaw over."

© Nitrome

33

En-Gen

To the right of Main Street stands the En-Gen power station, filled with hard-working, hard-hat wearing Roarkers. Dizzee Bolt and the other Roarkers spend their days **rotating the Blox** that produce Monstrowatts to keep everything in Monstro City running smoothly. It's up to you to help them!

Click the mouse on the joints between Blox to rotate the surrounding squares clockwise. When four Blox of the same colour meet, they **vaporize into energy**, filling up the gradually decreasing power bar.

Diamond Blox add **bonus points** to your energy. You can rack up combos by connecting groups of colours in one move. You can also gain combos when the Blox that fall to fill a gap create another group!

"Monstro City always needs more power, so pitch in with Dizzee Bolt, to give her Monstrowatts a much-needed boost!"

"It might take a while to get your head around how rotating squares work. You'll need to practise to learn the best ways to bring colours together. Blox at the sides and bottom of the screen are much harder to reposition than ones in the centre, as they can be part of less squares."

"Groups of four can be any shape you like - don't just try and match lines!"

"It's important to remember that your squares can only be rotated clockwise! Moving things around to the left takes much longer than joining colours on the right. And when time is running out, long rotations can spell game over!"

"Although you can move any square at any time, you should try to join colours in as few moves as possible. Don't waste valuable seconds moving a colour to the other side of the board to create a group."

GEN

Bjorn Squish

With an **appetite for construction**, Roarker Bjorn Squish is always on lunch break. By promising to bring extra sandwiches to work, he's gained special permission from his supervisor, Dizzee Bolt, to eat and eat the whole day through. Click on him when you spot him to jolt him out of his daydreams!

Ken Tickles

Ken Tickles isn't the happiest Roarker in Monstro City. Envious of his colleague, Bjorn Squish, he works twice as hard to be noticed, and still doesn't attract any attention. What we do notice is that three eyes are better than one when precision drilling is involved!

Safety First!

Ken Tickles needs to drill down through the road, but Bjorn didn't finish shutting off the water and electricity supplies before he went to lunch! Only one of these five drill spots is safe to use. Which is it?

A   **B**   **C**   **D**   **E**

Demolition City

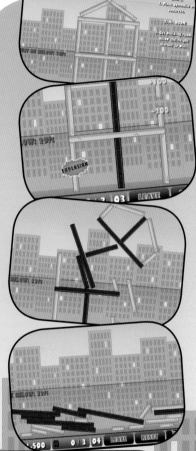

Twenty matchstick buildings have been scheduled for demolition across the city, and it's your job to **bring them down** whilst earning the most amount of money doing it!

Position the dynamite on the pillars before pressing the **Boom!** button. You'll need to reduce the building to a pile of rubble lower than the blue line to pass each level, but there are bonuses for getting it even lower. Don't forget to **watch out** for any nearby skyscrapers you need to avoid!

Only one stick of dynamite can be placed on each matchstick, and at the higher levels you'll have to deal with steel columns. These **cannot be destroyed** and are much sturdier than their wooden counterparts.

"Whilst you earn extra points for particularly destructive explosions, you'll gain even more for using fewer sticks of dynamite. Try and spot the pivotal points in each building that can knock the entire thing off balance."

"Steel pillars can remain standing even after everything around them has fallen down. Place your dynamite beneath them to send them tipping over."

© Armor Games

Time4Cat

A hungry cat has made its way onto a busy junction in **search of food**. Help it find a meal without getting stepped on by pedestrians!

Use the mouse to guide the cat from one piece of food to another, but be careful of the **careless passers-by**! They'll only move when you do, so make sure that your path doesn't cross theirs on the way to your next meal. The quicker you reach each piece of food, the more points you get, but the pedestrians will start walking faster as well.

You can also pick up white orbs that will push people out of your way with a click of your mouse, but use them carefully as you can only hold three at a time!

"The most direct route isn't always the safest, so don't be afraid to move in a different direction. This makes the passers-by walk on past your target and lets you reach it safely!"

"The longer you last, the more crowded the junction becomes. Don't be surprised if a few different types of traffic make an appearance! They'll move faster than the pedestrians, so be sure to factor that in."

© Megadev

Ice Breaker

A fleet of Viking longships has become lost in the frozen wastes. It's your job to **return each crew to its ship**.

Use the mouse to draw cuts in the ice to release the Vikings and send them sliding and falling back into the boat. You'll need to cut carefully to create a safe path and you only have **thirty cuts** to work with, so choose wisely!

As the levels progress, more environmental objects will appear, including swinging ropes and pivots, rocks with strange mystical properties, and even wild animals and exploding Viking women! Take the time to learn the **special properties** of each object and plan your route before making the first cut. The less cuts you use, the higher your score for each level.

"You'll often need to work around the Vikings rather than interact with them directly. Look carefully at the position of pivots and ropes. A careful cut can catapult your target directly into the longship!"

"Each longship has a captain whose hammer can smash smaller chunks of ice to release trapped Vikings. He will also destroy any enemies that happen to land in his boat, which is useful for clearing a path for the rest of his crew!"

© Nitrome

Rubble Trouble

In the middle of a busy city, a demolition crew is hard at work earning money. Help them **demolish their buildings** in the quickest and safest ways possible.

You'll be provided with a variety of tools to perform the job, including nitro for small explosions, cannonball-firing cement mixers, helicopters with wrecking balls and grabbing claws, and even an air strike and a missile launcher! It's important to use these tools carefully as often there are **additional objectives** to complete. Sometimes you'll need to rescue builders from the top of a derelict building, or retrieve money from the middle of a tower. There's nothing worse than dropping a ton of masonry on the nearby vase museum!

Take careful note of your surroundings and plan your demolition carefully before you begin. Often your tools will only have a limited number of uses, so don't waste them!

Play ►
Scores 🏆
Options ✕
Help ?
Credits ★

Drill time! Serious damage coming up boss

MINICLIP.COM

"When rescuing builders from the top of buildings, try to take out horizontal layers of masonry beneath them to stop their platform from tipping to one side!"

"The cement mixer cannon has a power bar that you can adjust with each shot. Often it's easier to be more precise with less power, so be careful when you release the mouse button!"

"Certain levels already have explosives built into the buildings, and you should target these first. Triggering one with a well-placed rocket can lead to a chain reaction that causes huge amounts of damage quickly."

© Nitrome

Gobtron

The **ancient monster** Gobtron has arisen from his slumber and discovered that the pesky nuisance known as 'man' wants to destroy him! So begins a war that spans humanity's history.

Click and pull back the **Snot Shot** hanging from Gobtron's nose to fire it towards the ground and snatch up the attacking humans. The more humans you grab in one go, the higher the DNA reward for catching them and the more weapons you'll be able to purchase to aid in Gobtron's fight. The **Booger Cannon** allows you to mark targets and blast them with a giant bogey. The **Bubble Shield** protects Gobtron's vulnerable belly and the disgusting **Sonic Burp** sends enemies flying!

Occasionally power-ups and other bonuses will pass across the top of the screen. Hit them with your Snot Shot or Booger Cannon to collect them and add even more oomph to your attacks!

"Don't forget you can buy upgrades to your existing powers with DNA. Extra health will help you survive the tougher enemies, whilst stickier snot will allow you to pick up more humans and increase your combos."

"The Booger Canon takes a little time to fire, so anticipate where your targets will be when it does and adjust your crosshairs accordingly!"

YOU WIN!

LEVEL SCORE 141
NEW DNA GAINED
LEVEL TOTAL 282
TOTAL DNA 282

PROCEED

© Juicy Beast

Flutterby Field

On the Port-side of Main Street lies the haven that is Flutterby Field. Or it would be if it hadn't been **infested with bugs**!

Luckily the Flutterbies have **Colonel Catcher** on their side, and he has bravely decided to step up to the challenge of rescuing them all. Armed with his trusty net, it's your job to use the mouse to guide him around the field. Click the left mouse button to **catch the Flutterbies** in his net so that he can move them to a less-infested spot!

You'll have to **move quickly** if you want to catch as many Flutterbies as possible, as they'll fly away from you the moment they see you. Different colours score different points, so try and net the rare multicoloured critters for maximum points.

But Flutterbies aren't your only worry in this game. Bugs of all shapes and sizes are constantly burrowing out of the ground, and if you touch one it'll give you a nasty bite. Colonel Catcher can only take a few bites before he loses his nerve and runs away, so try to avoid them as much as you can!

"Poor old Colonel Catcher - these Flutterbies don't realise that he's trying to help!"

"Practise using the controls and guiding Colonel Catcher on the easier difficulty before moving up to medium. Only the very brave can survive the hardest setting for very long!"

"Keep your mouse close to Colonel Catcher whilst guiding him around. It means that you can stop more quickly to line up your swipes!"

"Those bugs will chase you wherever you go, but don't worry, once you've been bitten you'll be indestructible for a few seconds, giving you enough time to escape to the other side of the field!"

Colonel Catcher

This old soldier has a **keen eye for nature** and is obsessed with pinning Flutterby species to his "Genus of Monstro City" whiteboard. Colonel Catcher retired early from his tour of Bendia, and can now be found roaming Flutterby Field with shouts of exasperation as he **tries to catch new beauties.** He is fiercely protective of the environment they inhabit. He worries that if anything should happen to disturb Flutterby Field, all the Flutterbies will fly away before he has the chance to discover an **entirely new species** and name it after himself.

Two of a Kind

Colonel Catcher is having trouble identifying his Flutterbies. Only two of these specimens are identical, but which are they?

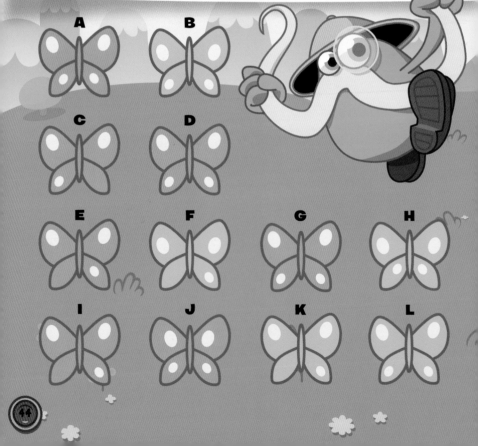

Hide Caesar II

Protect the **golden coin** from the grit being poured across the landscape by using all manner of metal and wood contraptions - then create your own!

From the moment the level starts, gravity will begin to take effect, and you'll need to **move quickly** to take advantage of the possible shelters available for the Caesar. Drop items from above to knock the coin or any of the objects around it, whilst making sure the Caesar doesn't go rolling off the screen. Once the last object has fallen, the grit will begin to fall, and if a piece touches the coin then you go back to the beginning of the level.

Once you've completed all the **fiendish puzzles** the game has to offer, why not **try creating your own** using the level editor? Place objects in the world and alter their properties to tweak how they behave, before giving the player their droppable objects. You can test it at any time to make sure everything is working as it should. When you're done, you can save it to **show your friends**!

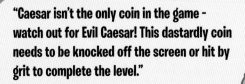

"Caesar isn't the only coin in the game - watch out for Evil Caesar! This dastardly coin needs to be knocked off the screen or hit by grit to complete the level."

45

© Gimme5Games

Feed the King

The hungry king has demanded that his chef bring him the **most cakes he can possibly carry**. But stacking such a huge pile is harder than it looks!

Press the down arrow key to drop cakes on top of each other as they move across the screen. **Bonus points** are awarded for landing cakes on the edges of others, placing a narrow-based cake on top of a narrow-topped cake, and squashing birds. But **beware**, if your stack hits a flying bomb or your cake misses the pile, then your multiplier will be lost.

There are three modes to choose from in this game:

Classic Mode
Provides you with three hearts, which are removed every time you drop a cake or explode a bomb. The round ends when all the hearts have been lost.

Time Mode
Asks you to stack as many cakes as possible in one minute. It won't punish you for dropping cakes, but their fall will lose you precious seconds as well as your score multiplier.

Cake Mode
Gives you fifty cakes and challenges you to arrange them into the highest score possible.

"Danger bonuses are awarded for piling your cakes close to a bomb without setting it off!"

"Rotten cakes appear in the classic mode and you'll need to drop those down the side of the pile to avoid losing a heart."

"You can earn bonus points at the end of each level. Steer the king using the left and right arrow keys as he chomps his way through the pile. The more cakes he eats in a row, the higher this score is multiplied."

© Juicy Beast

Spacetacular Voyage

Guide your spaceship through a universe of angry shapes using the mouse or arrow keys to **adjust the speed and direction** of your ship. Press the space bar to explode and create some breathing room, but remember, your **ship needs to recharge** before it can explode again.

Hitting the falling shapes won't hurt you. In fact, the more you hit and the harder you hit them, **the more points you'll receive**. However, if you're pushed to the bottom of the screen you'll die, and if you hit the top you'll bounce back. Careful flying is the key to victory!

"You can unleash your explosion before it's fully recharged, but its blast will be weaker."

"Take advantage of the slower-moving larger shapes to rack up some extra points by slamming into them."

"The nose of your ship is great for getting between shapes and prising them apart so you can squeeze through."

"The harder you hit the top edge of the screen, the further you'll bounce back. Try and keep your movement steady to avoid an early death."

© BitBattallion

47

Peppy's Stunt Bike

On the racetracks in front of Puzzle Palace, Peppy is preparing to wow the crowds with her insane **motorcycle stunts**!

Pick your track and get tricking to rack up enough combos to earn those **precious trophies**. There are three trophies for every level - bronze, silver and gold. The more you win, the more tracks you'll get to play with.

Use the X key to accelerate and the left and right arrow keys to turn your bike and **perform wheelies** or flips in the air. The C key is the stunt key. When you press it, it'll perform different tricks depending on your angle in the air. The up and down arrow keys will make Peppy switch between lanes.

Angling your bike will add height to your jumps. The **speed boosts** on the track will send you soaring into the air, where you can perform your most daring feats. Stars will add precious points to your score, but there are hazards on the track as well. Water, oil and sand will slow Peppy down to a crawl, and speed bumps will send you flying unless you lift your front wheel up in time to hop over them.

"Head over to **MoshiGames.com** to play this and loads of other great games!"

"A perfect landing is a great way to give your combo an extra multiplier. Simply land horizontally to add fifty points and an extra 'x1' to your score!"

"Even after you land, your combo multiplier will remain for a few seconds, which means that you can extend it even further by beginning another trick before it disappears. But there's a downside as well - if you crash before the combo is added to your score, you'll lose everything!"

"Keep your finger on the X key whilst you're in the air - it'll make you turn faster!"

"When the stars make a line across the tracks, try zigzagging across the lanes to grab more than one."

Peppy the Moshling

Peppy the Penguin Moshling is a flightless creature - until she gets on her motorbike! Even when she's not performing stunts over at the Moshi Games racetrack she always wears her crash helmet and goggles - just in case.

Peppy is a rare Moshling, but you can lure her to your garden by growing a combo of any Moon Orchid, yellow Magic Beans and a red Moon Orchid.

Donut Ninja

Help the ninja bear **defeat his evil opponents** by feeding them with donuts!

Click the bears as they descend to throw them a donut and send them flying away on their ninja kites. Some **greedy bears** need more than one donut to be satisfied, so keep an eye out for the number on their shirts to find out how many you need to throw. If a bear reaches the bottom of the screen then it's game over, so make sure you click the lowest ones first.

You can also get **bonus points** by clicking the strange UFOs that pass through the level, but don't let them distract you from the bears!

"Be careful with your aiming. You won't lose points if you miss a bear, but it will delay your next throw!"

© Tappi Bear

R. I. F. T.

Help this **loyal little robot** cross the gadgets and traps of his master's laboratory to bring him plenty of delicious cake!

Use the arrow keys to move and jump, and the S and X keys to grab hold of boxes, as you hold down switches and **dodge energy shots** to reach the precious cake. Once you get it, you'll need to find a safe route back to the master. Be careful: sometimes getting to the cake will be **too dangerous** even for your little robot! You'll need to do some careful planning to find a way to transport it over to your greedy master!

"Boxes are at the perfect height to absorb energy blasts, so use them as shields to cross treacherous areas. Without you holding them, the blasts will also push both the boxes and the cake along the floor. This should come in handy during the later levels!"

"There are lots of bonus tin cans dotted around each level, but they can often be dangerous to get to!"

"Most levels need things done in a certain order. Working out how to bring the cake to the master early on will stop you having to backtrack down dangerous pathways later!"

© Devm

Run Shelby Run

Returning home from his early morning jog, Shelby is overjoyed to discover that someone has **left him a present** by his postbox. But before he can open it, Ecto the Moshling **snatches it away!**

Help Shelby give chase across the snowy landscape by pressing the space bar to jump. His speed will decrease gradually over time and you'll need to collect as many sweets as possible to **speed him up** until he catches up with the jealous Moshling. But Ecto's friends aren't going to let the present go that easily and keep trying to slow Shelby down. If you don't dodge out of their way, Shelby will be knocked back into his shell and lose both speed and health. Collect hearts to **increase Shelby's health**, otherwise it's back to the beginning of the level.

If Shelby catches up with Ecto, then Ecto will toss the present to one of his friends. You'll need to catch up with all five of his friends to discover what's beneath the wrapping paper.

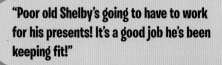

"Poor old Shelby's going to have to work for his presents! It's a good job he's been keeping fit!"

Shelby the Moshling

Shelby might look slow, but this **exercise-obsessed** Moshling won't let his shell slow him down! Every day he's up at the crack of dawn to put on his winged headband and go for an early morning run around Moshi Island, leaving him refreshed and ready for the day ahead!

Shelby will try anything to **beat his own time**, and the contents of his mysterious present could be just the thing to improve his performance . . .

To claim your exclusive virtual gift, go to the sign-in page of **MOSHIMONSTERS.COM** And enter the seventh word on the third line of the seventy-seventh page of this book! Your surprise free gift will appear in your treasure chest!

RAARGHLY'S TIPS

"You can find this game over at **Moshimonsters.com!**"

"It is impossible to dodge the oncoming Moshlings whilst under a platform, so try and take the high road whenever possible."

"By the time Shelby reaches the higher levels he's begun to tire and his speed will drop more rapidly than before. You'll need to collect several sweets in a row to pick up the pace!"

"The closer Shelby gets to catching his present, the less time he has to avoid the oncoming Moshlings - so keep your eyes peeled. If you have no hearts left, it's often better to drop behind to where you can avoid oncoming threats until you've regained some health."

The Underground Disco

Hidden beneath a manhole on Ooh La Lane, the exclusive **members-only** underground disco is always open!

Stroll past the flashing bulbs of the paparazzi to **strut your funky stuff** on the dance floor and try to impress the judges with your outrageous moves!

There are a lot of meters to pay attention to in this game, but the most important is the Track. As the song plays, coloured arrows will descend in time to the music. It's up to you to hit the correct arrow keys when they reach the bottom to execute the **perfect moves**.

To the right of the track is the Cheer-o-meter, which shows you just how well your dancing is going down with the crowd. The more notes you hit, and the more **"Excellent!"**s you get for perfect timing, the further this arrow will swing to the right. This makes the noise of the crowd grow even louder! But if you miss too many notes, they'll get bored and your monster will begin to stumble through his moves.

If you succeed in hitting more than ten notes in a row, the combo meter will appear. This multiplies your points until you miss a note or the song ends.

Once the song is over, it's time for the judges to **rate your performance**. You will be judged on how many notes you hit, how many "Excellent!"s you achieved, your longest combo and your overall score. A score of 20 or more means you passed the song! And the more songs you pass, the more songs you unlock!

"You can also reach the Underground Disco through the hollow tree stump on Main Street, the dancing garden shed on Sludge Street, and in a secret cave at the Port!"

"A musical ear will help you here. Use the rhythm of the song to help you time the quicker notes and get those 'Excellent!'s"

"Play through the 'easy' mode first. It'll get you used to the basics, and helps you to get a feel for the music without too many notes to worry about. Once you're familiar with the tracks, 'medium' will introduce you to chords (that's more than one arrow key at a time!), then 'hard' will challenge you to match the song almost note for note!"

"Get on down to the Underground Disco, where music is king and only the best dancers are allowed in!"

The Judges

Meet the trio every visitor to the Underground Disco wants to impress! If they like you, they'll give you new songs to perform to. If not, well, Simon never likes anyone anyway.

Roary Scrawl

Roary Scrawl tirelessly types away at *The Daily Growl* office, determined to keep Monstro City informed with all the ooze that's fit to print. With all those eyes, it's only natural that he's the **Editor-in-Chief**. He spends his free time searching for his misplaced eyeballs and snoop . . . er, monster-watching. In the evenings he likes to kick back and relax by heading down to the Underground Disco to check out the latest dancers. In a place as dynamic as the Underground Disco, there's always an ooze story by the end of the night!

Tyra Fangs

Runway model, TV show host, and **gossip queen**, Tyra Fangs hails from Goo York but now spends her days in Monstro City with her boyfriend Roary Scrawl. She loves facials, shopping, and bossing Roary around. She also loves **hanging out with the bands** at the Underground Disco, but sometimes Roary thinks the only reason she comes is to keep an eye on him!

Simon Growl

On the rare occasion that Simon Growl doesn't tell you what he really thinks, you can always look at his hair to find out how he feels. Despite being voted **meanest judge** three years in a row, Simon is still the greatest (and only!) **talent scout** in Monstro City. Notoriously hard to impress, only the greatest dancers receive a perfect ten from Simon - and those that do are sure to become Monstars!

But the Judges aren't the only people who help the Underground Disco remain the **fun-capital** of Monstro City, so spare a thought for the man at the door!

Bubba the Bouncer

Bubba is a prominent tattoo artist and **nightclub bouncer**. Working at the Underground Disco, and practising his moves at home on his Dance, Dance, Roarvolution machine, he hopes to show off his style in an **upcoming dance-off**, if he ever gets a day off.

Mr Runner

Mr Runner **loves to run**, even when his world is filled with deadly lava, treacherous ice and even zero gravity! Use the arrow keys to run, jump and slide through each stage and try to **beat the time** set for gold, silver and bronze medals. Collecting gold coins will reduce your time, but beware of the lava! One touch will send you back to the last checkpoint and lose you valuable seconds.

Once you've mastered the available stages (or decided that they're too hard!) why not **try making your own** using the level editor? Simply drag and drop different materials to create new obstacle courses to traverse!

MR RUNNER

PLAY
LOAD
CREATE

"Don't forget you can slide down walls. This will slow your descent and make it easier to time your jump away!"

"There are often several different routes through a level and several optional checkpoints along each one. Don't be afraid to try out a new direction to try and beat your time."

"If you get stuck on a level, move on to the next one! Two later levels are always unlocked ahead of your current stage."

Mushroomer

Help this plucky adventurer **harvest the mushrooms** that have been running wild through the forest by pushing blocks, opening pathways, avoiding traps and demolishing rocks with your hammer!

Use the arrow keys to move and jump, and the space bar to use your hammer, as you search out enough multicoloured fungi to exit the level. Small blocks can be demolished or pushed using your hammer whilst standing next to them. Big blocks take a harder blow, and can only be destroyed from above!

You may come across a number of **treasure chests** hidden away throughout the levels. Open them to gain **bonus points** or extra lives!

"Look before you leap! There are some sets of blocks that can only be crossed by one route. You don't want to end up stuck in a hole! If you do, press the R key to go back to the nearest checkpoint."

"Some mushrooms will try and escape, hopping away until they hit an obstacle. Be careful that they don't lead you into danger!"

"Almost every block has a purpose, even if you can't see it. A lucky push might open up a path to a chest or two further down the level!"

"Some blocks seem to hover in the air. Simply jump into them to drop them back to Earth!"

© Ant Karlov

Mining Truck

Help the dumper truck reach its destination with **as much cargo as possible**! The route to the pick-up point is **rough and treacherous**. Only the most skilful drivers will get their entire load back safely as they work against the ticking clock. Use the up and down arrow keys to accelerate and brake, and the right and left keys to keep your balance, as the truck bounces over the rocky ground.

Bonus points are awarded for getting to the drop-off point quickly, but remember that if you lose too much cargo along the way you'll have to restart the level!

"Practice makes perfect. Going slow might seem to be the most careful way to get to the end of the level safely, but some jumps need quite a run-up. Use the signs along your route to work out what's coming next. Try different methods to work out the best way across."

"Don't just wait for your truck to fill up with cargo at the beginning; steer forwards and backwards to make sure it's loaded safely. There's nothing worse than having everything fall out the moment you accelerate!"

© Ant Karlov

Ecto's Cave

Hidden on the opposite side of the sewers to the Underground Disco is Ecto's Cave, a **spooky dark tunnel** filled with bats and one lonely ghost.

Use your mouse to guide Ecto through the cave, **dodging the zigzagging bats** to grab point-boosting balls of ectoplasm. The longer you survive, the more points you get. Every ball grants you 100 more!

But watch out, Ecto only has **three lives**, and the bats are rather annoyed that he's haunting their home!

Ecto the Moshling

Ecto is a very rare Fancy Banshee, one of the **friendliest Moshlings** of all. When they're not drifting through walls in the dead of night, they float around collecting **Rox dust** to keep themselves glowing brightly. See if you can find the right combination of seeds to entice Ecto into your garden!

"Ecto's Cave is quite hard to find, so be sure to tell your friends to pay the lonely ghost a visit!"

RAARGHLY'S TIPS

"You don't need to collect all the floating balls to get a high score. Sometimes it's safer to hang back and let the timer gather points rather than rush into danger. But beware: the longer you survive, the more flighty those bats become!"

Air Traffic Madness

Take a seat in air traffic control to **make your airports safe** and accident-free! Use your mouse to draw paths for the various planes that come in to land. Make sure they head towards the correct runways and approach them in the right direction whilst **avoiding collisions** with other aircraft.

There are four different types of aircraft - airliners, private jets, seaplanes and helicopters. Each moves at a different speed and requires a different runway to land on.

The Level Mode asks you to land a certain number of aircraft each day, whilst the **Survival Mode** challenges you to land as many aircraft as you can before a crash occurs!

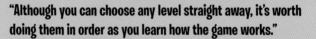

"Although you can choose any level straight away, it's worth doing them in order as you learn how the game works."

"A direct route isn't always the safest. Don't worry if you need one of your aircraft to circle as it waits for another to land!"

"Don't worry if your flight paths cross. As long as you get your timings right, they should be able to pass each other safely!"

© Kill5Games

Cargo Bridge

Balance the beams with your books to get your workmen across the deadly drops to **retrieve their cargo**.

Build bridges by clicking and dragging walkways with supports to form connections across each chasm. But bridges don't come cheap. You'll need to use all your planning skills to **create a structure** you can afford that is strong enough to hold an elephant!

Every dollar you don't spend on each level is stashed away for **challenge mode**, where you use the money you have left to build the longest bridge possible!

This is the design area where you will build your bridge. Each bridge element costs money and you have a limited budget. Your money amount is displayed in the upper-right corner of the screen.

Close   Next >>

"Experiment! Keep switching between your construction mode and test mode to find out just how many supports each bridge needs. If you've spent all your money on one bridge and can't afford another, take out a few beams to see if your workmen can still cross safely."

"Make your curves shallow. If your bridge is too steep it will take your workmen much longer to get over. This means that they're more likely to bunch up and bring the whole structure crashing down!"

"Triangles are your friend. Use plenty of supporting zigzags to spread the weight evenly."

Neon Rider

In the **virtual world**, nothing is solid unless you choose it to be. **Guide the neon biker** across the winding wireframe course using the W and S keys to control the speed, and the A and D keys to control your angle in the air. Perform tricks and stunts, but watch out: your biker can only travel along lines of the same colour as itself. Use the arrow keys to switch between blue, red, green and yellow lines whilst you race across the digital landscape in search of the **fastest time** and precious bonus points.

"Be quick with your colour changes. One wrong switch and you could end up falling to your doom, or stuck halfway through a now-solid wall!"

"Blue lines can be travelled whilst your bike is any colour, so use them to prepare for the next line change! Your map in the corner of the screen is great for seeing what obstacles are coming up."

"If you're having trouble climbing the steeper hills, tilt forward with the D key to accelerate even faster!"

© Armor Games

KiwiTiki

KiwiTiki's chicks have run amok! Help her call them home by using only one click!

Position KiwiTiki amongst her chicks and click to have her **call out** in an expanding circle. When a chick is caught by her call, they too will call out to catch others nearby, setting off a ripple effect amongst the flock. Each level gets **harder and harder**, asking you to catch even more chicks, so you'll need to position yourself carefully to get the **ripple effect** to catch them all!

Every level you complete gets you **1000 points**. If you catch more chicks than the target, you'll get another 1000 points for every extra chick! But beware, if your click fails to catch enough, you'll have five hundred points deducted from your score, so click carefully!

"Watch the movement of the chicks carefully and take your time. Eventually you'll find a moment where most of them begin to walk towards a central point and you can click there."

"Try and set off a chain reaction that traps the chicks in corners, where they're more likely to walk into the ripples."

"Try and click as far away from your chicks as possible without missing them! That way your first set of ripples will be more spread out and cover more ground."

© Dijiko

Flashcat

Help this heroic cat ride its bug-mobile across the neon race tracks that thread above the feline metropolis below and **foil an alien invasion** along the way!

Use the arrow or W, A, S and D keys to steer and hop your way across the track. Press the space bar to activate any of the **special abilities** you'll pick up along the way. Shoot cracked walls and enemies with the Bug Blaster or **clear the track** with a Shockwave. Megabounce across the larger gaps or Turbo your way closer to the finish line. Finally, invincibility will come in handy when the enemy aliens begin to increase in numbers.

There are also tons of score pick-ups and boost nodes to hit along the way. Springboards at the end of track sections will throw you high into the air whilst you search for a place to land!

© Nitrome

"Hitting enemies or walls won't kill you, but will slow you down. This reduces your final score and makes it harder to make those longer jumps."

"Often you're only given just enough power-ups to survive, so don't waste them!"

Phage Wars

The parasites are at war! Choose your species and guide it along the path to domination by infecting cells and **wiping out your enemies**.

You'll start each level with one cell that gradually fills with parasites. Click on it and drag your mouse over to another cell to send half of the parasites over to attack. Cells have a natural **immunity to parasites**, so will absorb a few before you can infect them, but once you've broken in they'll begin to produce even more parasites. You can select up to eight of your own cells to **launch large attacks** from all sides, or redistribute the parasites amongst the cells you already have.

Your enemies are also on a mission of infection though, and it's up to you to prevent them spreading by taking over the cells that they've possessed. But remember to leave some parasites behind to defend those you already have - the tables can turn quickly in this game.

"At higher levels you won't be able to see how many parasites your enemy's cells have. Keep an eye on the number of parasites they send out to attack you to make a rough guess."

"Larger cells tend to produce parasites more quickly, but the more smaller cells you possess, the less chance you'll have of being wiped out in one go."

"Choose your parasite wisely: each has different attributes that can affect how quickly they travel to other cells, or how many parasites it takes to destroy them."

PUZZLE PALACE

On a hill overlooking Monstro City, sits the Puzzle Palace - a jewel-encrusted marvel that houses loads of **brain-straining puzzles!**

Every day, it offers Monsters a Daily Challenge using a selection of puzzles from the ones your monster has unlocked! If you succeed, then you'll be rewarded with a **shower of Rox!**

There are a huge variety of puzzles available to you, and more are unlocked every time you level up! Aside from the **daily challenges,** you can try your hand at all of the individual puzzle types for bonus Rox - but you'll only get Rox on your first go each day. Your scores are recorded over time and you will see your highest score and average score after every round.

There are sixteen brain-training puzzles to choose from initially, but as your monster levels up, more will become available. Here are **Raarghly's tips** on his favourite ones.

RAARGHLY'S TIPS

"Try not to guess the answers to the Math Mash or Next Number puzzles. Each wrong answer removes a chunk of your time, so it's better to spend a few seconds working it out than just guessing!"

"In Secret Word you're asked to find a word amongst a grid of letters. The easiest way to do this is to use the answers! It's much quicker to go through the options one by one to see if they're there, rather than looking for the words hidden in the grid then checking to see if they're right!"

"You can use the same tactic in Alphabet Soup, which asks you which letter is missing from the jumble. Rather than finding out all the letters that are there, you only need to check which one of the answers isn't."

"Scare Squares is unlocked at level three, and asks you how many squares are in the picture. It will often overlap two squares to make another, so make sure you count that one as well!"

"Master of Moshi asks you questions about loads of items found all over Monstro City, so you'll need to do lots of exploring to find the correct answers to all of them!"

What's the total?

18-2

11	13
15	16

What word is hidden in the grid?

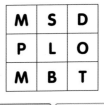

M	S	D
P	L	O
M	B	T

DOT	YES
ALL	SIT

Which letter of the alphabet does not appear here?

A	B	C	D	E
F	G	H	I	J
K	L	M	N	O
P	Q	R	T	U
V	W	X	Y	Z

G	S
L	O

How many squares are there?

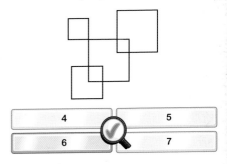

4	5
6	7

Star Ponies

"Do you have star power? Head over to **MoshiGames.com** to find out in this puzzle game that's harder than it looks!"

This game is simple to understand and easy to control, but **hard to master!** Use the arrow keys or the mouse to direct each star segment to any of the four targets to try and **build up full stars**. Points are awarded for completed stars. If you succeed in creating a perfect star (one made from a single colour), then **bonus points** will be awarded.

Think carefully about where you position each segment. If you try to position one over a target that already contains that piece then you'll lose a life, but if you wait too long and the stars around the middle fill up then you'll also lose a life. If you lose all four lives then the game is over, so you'll need to work quickly and carefully to gain the highest scores!

The Moshlings

The star power game has attracted some star powered Moshlings!

Priscilla

Priscilla's personality matches her hair - confident and fiery! You can attract her to your garden with two Moon Orchids of any colour and a yellow Snap Apple.

Gigi

This young unicorn Moshling is very shy and that makes her ultra rare! A blue Hot Silly Pepper, a red Moon Orchid and a yellow Hot Silly Pepper might lure her out though.

"The busier the board the harder it might be to find a slot for each new star segment. But don't worry, you'll never get a segment that won't fit. You just need to spot the slot before the timer runs out!"

"It's not just perfect stars that will give you a bonus. If you create a star where half the segments are the same colour, you'll get an extra 100 points. You also get another 100 when three-quarters of the star is the same."

"Whilst perfect stars give you a double score, you can often complete more multicoloured stars in the time it takes to find all the segments! Try and work towards one perfect star at a time and use the other three slots to complete as many stars as possible to get the highest scores."

⭐ MAKE STARS!
⭐ ARROW OR MOUSE CLICKS TO MOVE
⭐ WATCH THE TIMER
⭐ COMPLETE THE STAR IN THE SAME COLOR TO SCORE BONUS POINTS

START GAME!

Mr Snoodle

Mr Snoodle used to be embarrassed about his nose - until he realised how useful it is for sniffing out flowers. His favourite combination is any Hot Silly Pepper, a yellow Dragon Fruit and a purple Hot Silly Pepper.

Angel

With a unicorn horn and wings, you might expect Angel to be a bit of a show-off, but actually she's one of the friendliest Moshlings around. Get to know her by growing any Hot Silly Pepper, any Magic Beans and another Hot Silly Pepper of any colour.

More Fun at the Fun Park
Coming Soon

So you've visited Giuseppe Gelato's Ice Scream Parlour, you've raced Weevil Kneevil down his treacherous hill, you've unlocked every song at the Underground Disco and you've played every game in the Moshi Fun Park (What? Really? All of them? To the end? Wow). Well, that might sound like you've **played every game** there is to play, mightn't it?

Think again.

The Roarkers who work tirelessly to keep Monstro City running are always coming up with **new puzzles and adventures** to keep themselves – and you – entertained. If ideas were Monstrowatts then the Roarkers would power the whole of Monstro City with their crazy imagination, and the Fun Park is constantly being expanded to include more and more games!

It's always worth checking in to see **what's new**, and in the meantime you've still got Daily Challenges at the Puzzle Palace, with new games to unlock as you level up, and those Rox you've earnt helping out at Giuseppe's Ice Scream Parlour and the En-Gen power station could be used to buy one of Raarghly's Starcade Machines to turn your room into a gamer's paradise.

And Simon Growl is still waiting to give someone a perfect ten!

In Monstro City, the fun never stops, and the games are **just beginning**!

"When you become a Moshi Monsters member, you'll get access to all sorts of extra games and activities. With a Moshi Passport you can gain entry to the Underground Disco and buy games from me at the Starcade!"

"You've finished the book! You must be as skilled a gamer as me by now!"

"Visit the Daily Growl's offices and check out my good friend Roary Scrawl's blog to find out all the latest news on games and everything else to do with Moshi Monsters!"

"If you want to play even more games, check out **MoshiGames.com** where I've gathered together all of my favourites, plus loads that you won't find in Monstro City!"

"You can even let the friendly Roarkers who make **MoshiGames.com** know which games you like best by emailing them at hello@moshigames.com! They're always keen to know what you think!"

If your monster ever gets bored of waiting for you to finish at the Fun Park, head over to **MoshiGames.com** to play in peace! On this site you'll find loads of new and exclusive games, as well as your old favourites from the Fun Park. Exciting new games are being added all the time!

Be sure to keep checking in to see the latest additions as they arrive. The Game of the Day might just remind you of a forgotten classic that's due for a replay!

Making Mini Games

"Now that you've seen all the wonderful ideas our Roarkers have come up with, maybe it's time to try thinking about designing your own game! Over the next few pages are some hints and tips on how to begin putting together an idea that might one day end up in the Moshi Fun Fair!"

A Hero

First of all you need a hero - someone for the player to be as they explore your game - and it can be **anything you like**! Maybe you think your monster has a thirst for wacky adventures, or maybe you have a new monster in mind. It could even be a game about one of the characters you've met on your journey around Moshi Island!

The important part is that it needs to be someone the player cares about, someone they **want to succeed**. Think who you'd like to play as, and what that monster would be like. Why would you like to play as them? And why would other players?

Santa Claws
Possible hero? I think not.

An Adventure

'Adventure' is a grand word, but in reality it can be **as small or as epic as you like**. All games need a goal - something to try and achieve - even if it's just the next level or a higher score! Is your hero out to rescue a princess? Or defend a space station from invading aliens? Or are they simply trying to stop their garden being overrun by weeds?

This adventure needs to be exciting and new because that's what will make your game stand out from the crowd. If you see a game that you like in the Fun Park, try and work out what its adventure is, and see how it is used to **create puzzles**. Even a simple game like finding pairs can be turned into an adventure. How about finding the matching weedkiller to get rid of those pesky weeds we talked about earlier?

A Game Mechanic

"Try combining your adventure ideas with different types of game mechanics to come up with a winning formula!"

It sounds awfully technical, doesn't it? But it's the most **important part** of the process. Whilst the hero and the adventure are the hook that draws people in, the game mechanic is what **keeps them playing** (even when they should be doing their homework!). It needs to be **simple and easy to understand**, but as the game goes on it needs to be applied to more challenging situations as players get used to how the mechanic works and want to try using it in different ways. In Ecto's Cave you need to stop Ecto from hitting the bats by steering around them with the mouse. It's a simple mechanic, but one that **gets harder** as more and more bats fill the screen and begin zigzagging in all directions.

In Giuseppe's Ice Scream Parlour you have to hand out ice screams to loads of different customers, making sure that none of them go home unhappy. But if you **take that idea and mix it** with a different adventure it could become something else entirely. For example, you could be defending a castle from attack using three cannons pointing in different directions - but all of them need cannonballs and gunpowder to fend off the attacks from all sides. It's your job to make sure all the cannons have enough cannonballs to scare away the enemy, but not so many that another cannon cannot fire. At its core, this idea simply replaces Giuseppe's customers with cannons, and the ice screams with cannonballs, and turns it into a **completely new game**!

An Art Style

Now it's time to add the **finishing touches** to your game idea. The art style represents the whole look and feel of the game, building atmosphere and **setting the mood**. If your game is about a lone monster hunting for a long lost treasure, you'll want it to look very different to a funny game about delivering newspapers! So how do you want it to look? Cartoony? Or gritty? Colourful? Or black and white? Do you want the music to be bouncy and cheerful or loud and scary, or do you want no music at all and just the sound of wind and footsteps to accompany your hero?

It's also important to think about **how you want your player to feel** whilst they're playing this game. A mini game is often played in short bursts, so a grim, scary atmosphere is often hard to build up over such a small period of time, but it might also **make people want to keep playing** to the end to find out if the hero is all right. On the other hand, a fun, cheerful art style might make it easier for a player to keep coming back for that little burst of happiness inbetween doing other things (homework again, probably).

Play It

It might sound obvious, but now that you've **finished your game** - with your lovable hero and exciting combination of adventure and mechanic all wrapped up in the perfect art style - you need to play it! **Is it fun**? Does it work? Is it too hard, or too easy? Is there anything you should add or take away?

The answers to these questions will provide you with more help on making games than anything written in these pages and could **provide inspiration** for a whole new game you'd never even thought of! And also, let's be honest, what's the point of making games if you can't enjoy them yourself?

Happy gaming!

"Don't forget, when you make games they're not just for you, they're for your friends as well. Try asking them what they'd like to see in a game and see if you can design something that would make them happy!"

My Scores

Use these pages to make a note of your first scores on each game, and once you've mastered each one there's also room to record those extra special high scores!

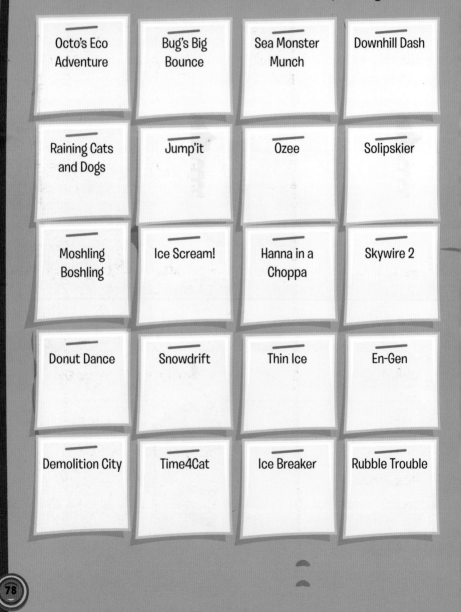

Octo's Eco Adventure

Bug's Big Bounce

Sea Monster Munch

Downhill Dash

Raining Cats and Dogs

Jump'it

Ozee

Solipskier

Moshling Boshling

Ice Scream!

Hanna in a Choppa

Skywire 2

Donut Dance

Snowdrift

Thin Ice

En-Gen

Demolition City

Time4Cat

Ice Breaker

Rubble Trouble

Gobtron

Flutterby Field

Hide Caesar II

Feed the King

Spacetacular Voyage

Peppy's Stunt Bike

Donut Ninja

R.I.F.T.

Run Shelby Run

The Underground Disco

Mr Runner

Mushroomer

Mining Truck

Ecto's Cave

Air Traffic Madness

Cargo Bridge

Neon Rider

KiwiTiki

Flash Cat

Phage Wars

Star Ponies

Answers

Page 9
Frazzled!

Octo's Eco Adventure - 700 Rox
Weevil Kneevil Downhill Dash - 950 Rox
Bug's Big Bash - 500 Rox
Sea Monster Munch - 850 Rox

Page 11
Raining Rubbish

35 eco-points

Page 13
Reach for the Sky

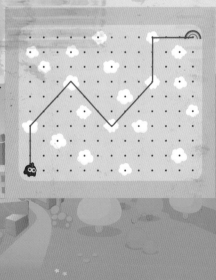

Page 15
The Terrible Tangle

E is the single sea monster

Page 17
The Rickety Tower

1. A, 2. K, 3. B, 4. I.

Page 27
Orders Up!

C and E can be served.

Page 36
Safety First!

D is the safe place to drill.